Sew! It! Doll Fashion!

D.I.Y. Doll Fashion and Accessories for the 'Me' Made Life

Here's what's inside:

Written and Illustrated
by
Ellen Lumpkin Brown

Those amazing pictures are by AVBrown Photography, Newark NJ

This book is dedicated to my family. They are always in my corner.

Written, published, and printed in the U.S.A.

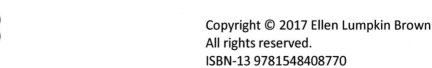

Copyright © 2017 Ellen Lumpkin Brown
All rights reserved.
ISBN-13 9781548408770
ISBN-10 1548408778

Hello There! I'm Ellen. I wrote *Sew! It! Doll Fashion!* It's a fun, new approach to create stylish clothes and accessories for your favorite 18-inch doll. If you already know your way around a sewing machine, this is just the book for you. It comes from my experience teaching tweenagers who love to DIY, want to show their own fashion independence and style, and live the me-made life. There are over a dozen cute projects that are super easy to sew. I loved designing these patterns and I hope you'll love stitching them up.

Live the 'Me' made life and let sewing be your super power!

THE DANDY DOZEN
Tools and Equipment

	Craft Iron		Pencils Pens and Marking Tools		Seam Ripper
	Needles and Pins and Pin Cushion		Fabric Glue and Glue Guns		Fray Check
	Inexpensive Test Fabrics		All- purpose Thread		Tape Measurer
	Sharp Scissors		Rulers		Elastic

For those stitching with metric measures, one inch equals 2.54 centimeters and one yard equals .91 meters.

How to Use Sew! It! Doll Fashion!

This book is filled with fun, easy-to-sew projects to stitch up for your dolls. All the projects are made with very simple shapes and mainly straight lines. Options are included so that you can personalize your creations for uniquely stylish results.

The patterns are designed to fit many popular 18-inch to 20-inch dolls. The last step of each project is to try the garment on your doll. You can adjust the back closure, drawstrings or elastic as needed to fit your doll perfectly.

I use a ¼" seam allowance for all of the patterns and it's already included either in the pattern itself or in the measurements provided at the beginning of each project. Just copy the pattern, cut out and you're ready to begin the project. All measurements are in inches.

When I'm designing fashions, I always use inexpensive test fabric or scraps to tryout my ideas. It's also a great way for you to make sure you understand how the pattern goes together before you cut that piece of fabric that you really love. You can make your own fabric stash for your doll clothes tryouts for free! Just collect old, worn out clothing, sheets, pillow cases and things like that. You can recycle them for your test sewing.

I also use a few of my favorite techniques from my tween clothing patterns and dollmaking patterns that are really great for making doll clothes too. Here are a few:

❖ The Ladder Stitch – this is a handy sewing stitch that is amazing for connecting two pieces of fabric together by hand invisibly! Here is how to do it:

The Ladder Stitch

Thread a hand needle with strong thread with a knot at one end. Bring the edges of the project opening close to each other. Make a small running stitch on one side of the opening. Make a second stitch on the other side of the opening. Continue alternating the sides of the stitching for five to six stitches; your sewing should look a little like the rungs of a ladder. Pull thread gently to close the seam. Continue to stitch until the closure is complete. Knot off.

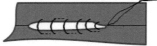

❖ Pressing your project as you go through the steps will give you a great result. Try using a craft iron. Its small size is great for doll seams. Make sure to use the type with lower heat settings.
❖ Draw a sewing line to help get your seams nice and straight.
❖ The Tools and Supplies page has my suggestions for a great doll clothing sewing kit!

Finally, every project has a skill level: one machine for beginning sewists and two machines for confident beginners. All of the projects are equally easy to stitch by hand or by machine.

Applique	Small piece of fabric sewn to the right side of project to create a design		**Stay Stitch**	Sewing through one layer of fabric. Usually to stabilize and keep the fabric from stretching or raveling	
Hem	Folding, pressing and stitching the raw edge of fabric to the wrong side		**Seam Allowance**	The distance between the stitching and the fabric edge	
Casing	A fabric tunnel for elastic or drawstring		**Selvage**	The factory finished edge of fabric	
Right Side (RS)/Wrong Side (WS)	RS - Side of fabric that will show on the outside. WS - side of fabric on the inside of the project.		**Baste**	Longest straight stitch on sewing machine. For temporary sewing or gathering.	
Clipping Corners	Cutting off a small amount of fabric to reduce bulk		**Backstitch**	Sewing in reverse. Usually five stitches to secure seam.	
Interfacing	Stabilizing fabric used on the wrong side of project for shaping		**Lengthwise Grain**	Weave of fabric running parallel to selvage	
Topstitching	Sewing on the outside of the project. Often decorative		**Crosswise Grain**	Weave of fabric running perpendicular to selvage	

Square Neckline Pocket Dress

You will need:
- 1/3 yd (m) of 45"-wide fabric
- Small scraps for the pockets
- One 6" piece of hook and loop tape
- One 24" piece of 3/8-inch wide ribbon (optional)

Skill Level

Square Neck Pocket Dress

Cut out back and front of the dress following the layout for the Applique Jumper.

Cut two pocket pieces.

1. Finish the Neckline. Make a small clip at each corner of the neck edge. Fold a narrow ¼-inch hem. Stitch in place.

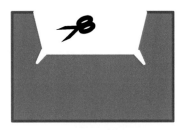 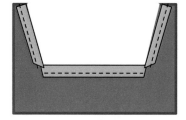

2. Finish the back. Fold a narrow ¼-inch hem along the back edges. Stitch in place

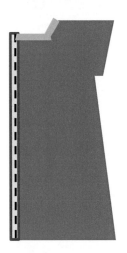

3. Make the pockets. Fold a narrow ¼-inch hem on three sides of the pocket. Leave the top edge raw as shown. Stay stitch across the top edge.

4. Position the pockets on the front of the dress as shown. Stitch close to the edge on three sides.

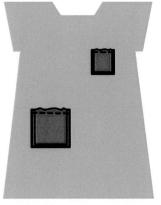

5. Make the shoulder seams and finish the Cap Sleeve. Fold a narrow ¼-inch hem at the edge of the armhole. Stitch in place.

 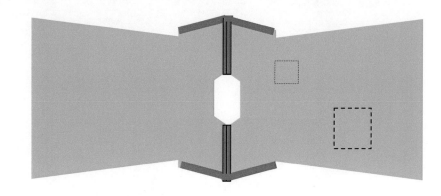

6. Sew the side seams.

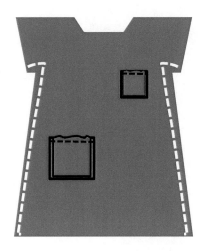

7. Try the dress on your doll. Mark the placement for hook and loop tape or snaps along the back closing.

Mark the hem. Cut your dress so that one inch remains below the hemline. Fold a ½-inch hem.   Press. Fold a second ½ -inch hem. Press and stitch in place.

That's it!

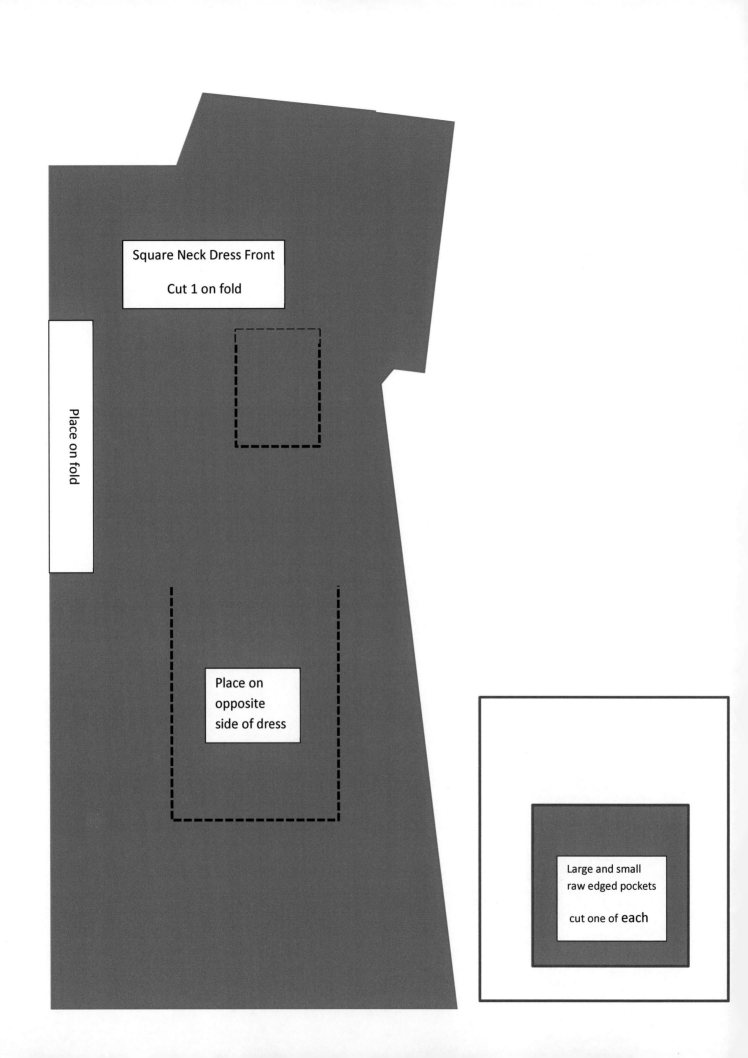

Square Neck Dress Front

Cut 1 on fold

Place on fold

Place on opposite side of dress

Large and small raw edged pockets

cut one of **each**

Square Neck Dress Back

Cut 2

The Versatile City Sandal

You'll need

- Two 6" x 6" scraps
- 6"x6" piece of interfacing
- 1.5 yards of 3/8-wide ribbon.

A chopstick

Skill Level:

City Sandals

Cut out pattern piece (p.45). Stack your fabric with the right sides together and the interfacing on the bottom. Trace the pattern piece on the top layer of fabric.

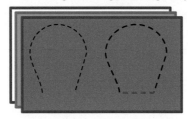

Stitch around the sole leaving straight edge open.

Cut out, leaving a 1/8-inch seam allowance.

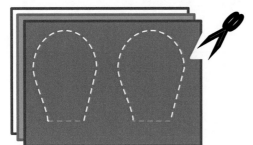

Turn right side out and smooth with a chopstick.

Grab the ribbon. Cut a 3-inch piece. Fold in half. Sew across leaving a ½-inch loop. Fold the raw edges of the sandal inward. Insert the loop tails into the sandal. Stitch across the opening to hold securely.

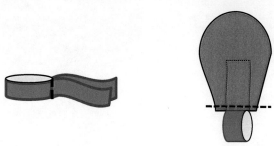

Cut a second piece of ribbon 12 inches long. Fold in half to find the center. Position the center on the top of the sandal Stitch in place securely by stitching a rectangle or reversing twice.

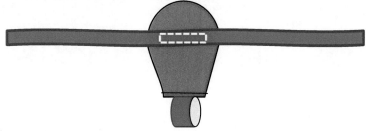

Wrap the ribbon around the front of the doll's foot so that it fits nicely.

Bring each of the remaining ends of the ribbon through the loop. Stitch in place by hand. Tie the ends in a bow. Cut away the excess ribbon.

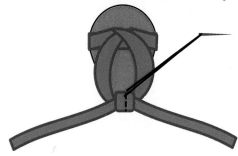

Halter Drawstring Dress and Carryall

You will need:
¼ yd of fabric
One scrap 15" x 2" for the
shoulder strap.
One large safety pin

Skill Level

Halter Draw String Dress

Cut out the pattern piece. You may also use ½ inch wide ribbon for the strap. Follow the layout for the Applique Jumper for the front. The back is a 7.5x7.5 inch square.

Make the armholes. Turn a double hem along the edges of the front above the clip mark to create the armhole.

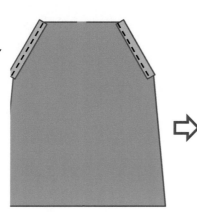

Make the neckline casing. Fold a narrow ¼-inch hem at the top of the front of the dress. Fold a second hem that is 5/8-inch wide. Press. Stitch in place.

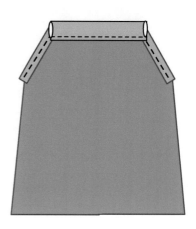

Make the back of the dress. Fold and stitch a casing at the top of the skirt just like you just completed for the front.

Insert the elastic following the steps of the hand sew skirt on p. 44.

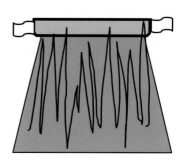

Put the back and front together with the right sides touching. Stitch one side seam.

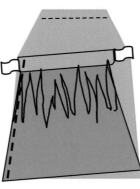

Fold and sew a double ½-inch hem.

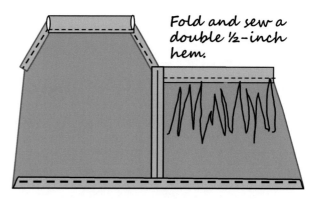

Pin and stitch the remaining side seam

To make the tie:

Fold the tie lengthwise. Press.

Open and fold the two raw edges to meet.

Fold again so that the edges are enclosed. Press,

Stitch through all layers.

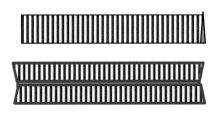

Attach the strap to a large safety pin. Insert the strap into the back casing and then through the front casing. Tie a small knot at each end of the strap.

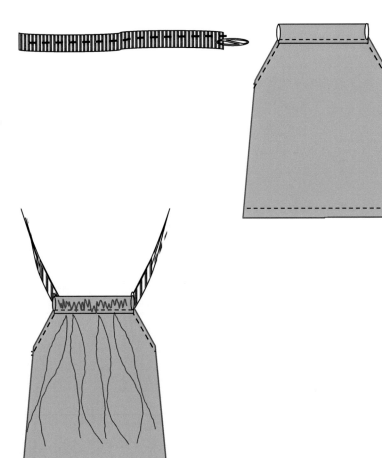

That's it! Try the dress on your doll. Tie halter at the neck.

Optional — add a raw edged pocket. Cut out the pocket pattern for the square neck dress.. Position on the front of the dress as marked on the pattern. Sew along three sides leaving the top edge open.

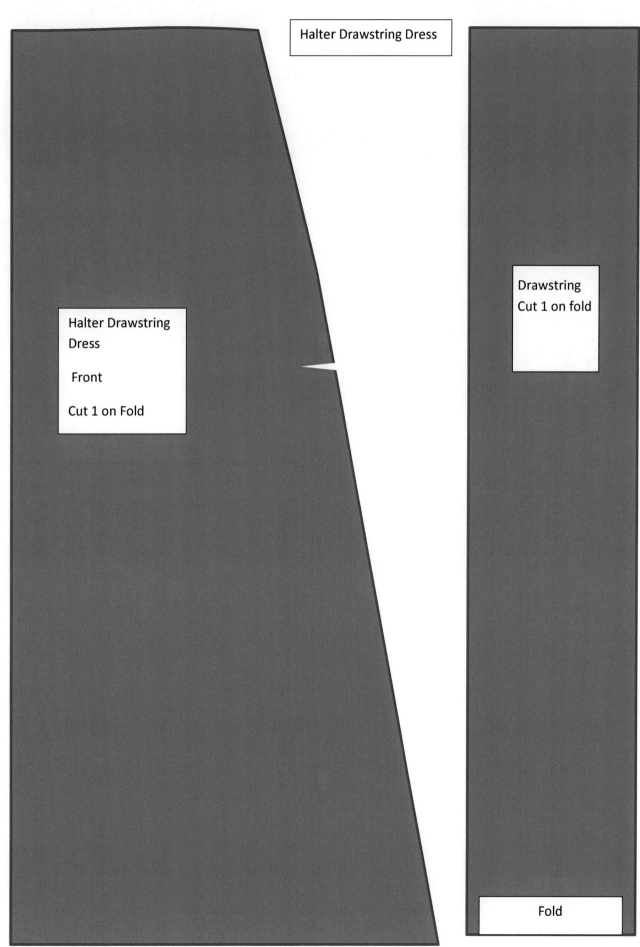

Halter Drawstring Dress

Halter Drawstring
Dress

Front

Cut 1 on Fold

Drawstring
Cut 1 on fold

Fold

14

Make a Quick Carryall

Cut one piece of fabric 10" x 5".
Optional: One piece of lining fabric 10" x 5".

Cut an 8 inch long piece of ½ inch ribbon.

Skill Level: Beginner

1. Fold a narrow ½ inch hem along each short edge of the fabric. Stitch in place.

2. Fold the fabric in half as shown. Sew a ½ inch seam along each side.

3. Turn right side out

4. Pin the ribbon strap over the seam on the inside of the bag. Sew in place by hand. You can stop here or you can line the bag.

5. To line the Carryall, repeat steps 1 and 2. Insert the lining into the outer bag with the wrong sides together. Stitch together at the top of the bag by hand or machine.

More Options: Applique a heart or add a pocket at step 2.

Two Toned Shorts

You will need:
- ¼ yd (m) of fabric
- A small scrap of fabric for the contrasting shorts leg
- 11 inches of ½-inch wide elastic

Large safety pin

Skill Level

Two-Tone Shorts

Cut out the Shorts Pattern piece. Stack two contrasting pieces of fabric and pin the pattern piece on top. Cut out the shorts.

Make the casing. Turn a narrow ¼-inch hem at the top of each shorts piece. Fold a second time with a ¾-inch hem. Stitch in place.

Hem the shorts. Turn a double ¼-inch hem at the bottom of each shorts piece. Sew in place.

Insert the elastic. Cut two pieces of ½-inch elastic to 5.5 inches. Attach a large safety pin or other insertion tool and insert the elastic into the casing.

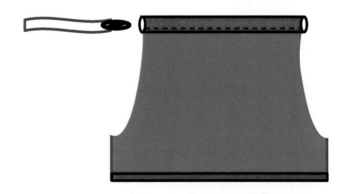

Stitch at each end of the casing to hold the elastic in place.

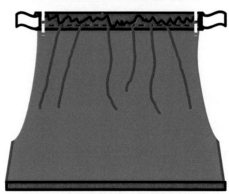

Put the shorts with the right sides together and stitch the curved crotch seam on each side. Make sure to back stitch over the elastic for extra security.

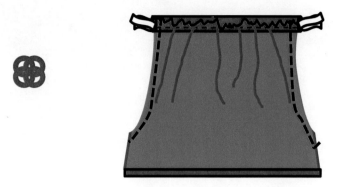

Sew the in-seam. Match the crotch seams together. Pin the inseam and sew from one hemmed edge to the crotch seam. Then sew from the other hemmed edge to the crotch seam.

That's it! Try the shorts on your doll!

Shorts

Front and Back

Cut 2

T-Shirt (with or without sleeves)

Cut a piece of fabric 12" x 12". Fold in half with the right sides together. Cut out the T-shirt pattern piece. Pin the pattern to the fabric to hold it in place. Trace the pattern with a pencil or fabric marker.

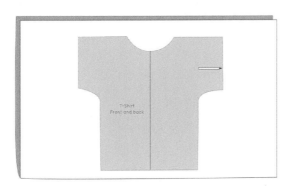

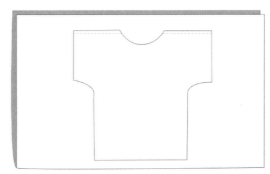

1. Stitch Shoulder Seams. Just place the edge of the presser foot on the line you have traced. The seam is sewn on the inside of this line. Cut the T-shirt out on the line you've traced.

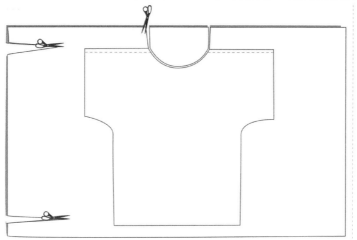

2. Fold one side of the T-Shirt in half to find the center. Cut the T-Shirt open as shown. This will be the back of the Top.

3. Hem sleeves or armholes, if sleeveless, with a narrow hem **OR** simply stay stitch and cut away the excess fabric. You can finish the neckline by hand OR by using the stay stitch cut away technique.

4. Sew the side seams.

5. Try your T-shirt on your doll. Mark placement for hook and loop tape or snaps for closing. Sew or glue small pieces of hook and loop tape or one narrow strip of hook and loop tape for the back closing. Or, sew on snaps for the back closure.

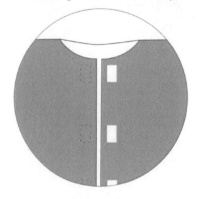

6. That's it! You've created the T-Shirt!

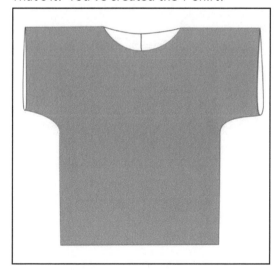

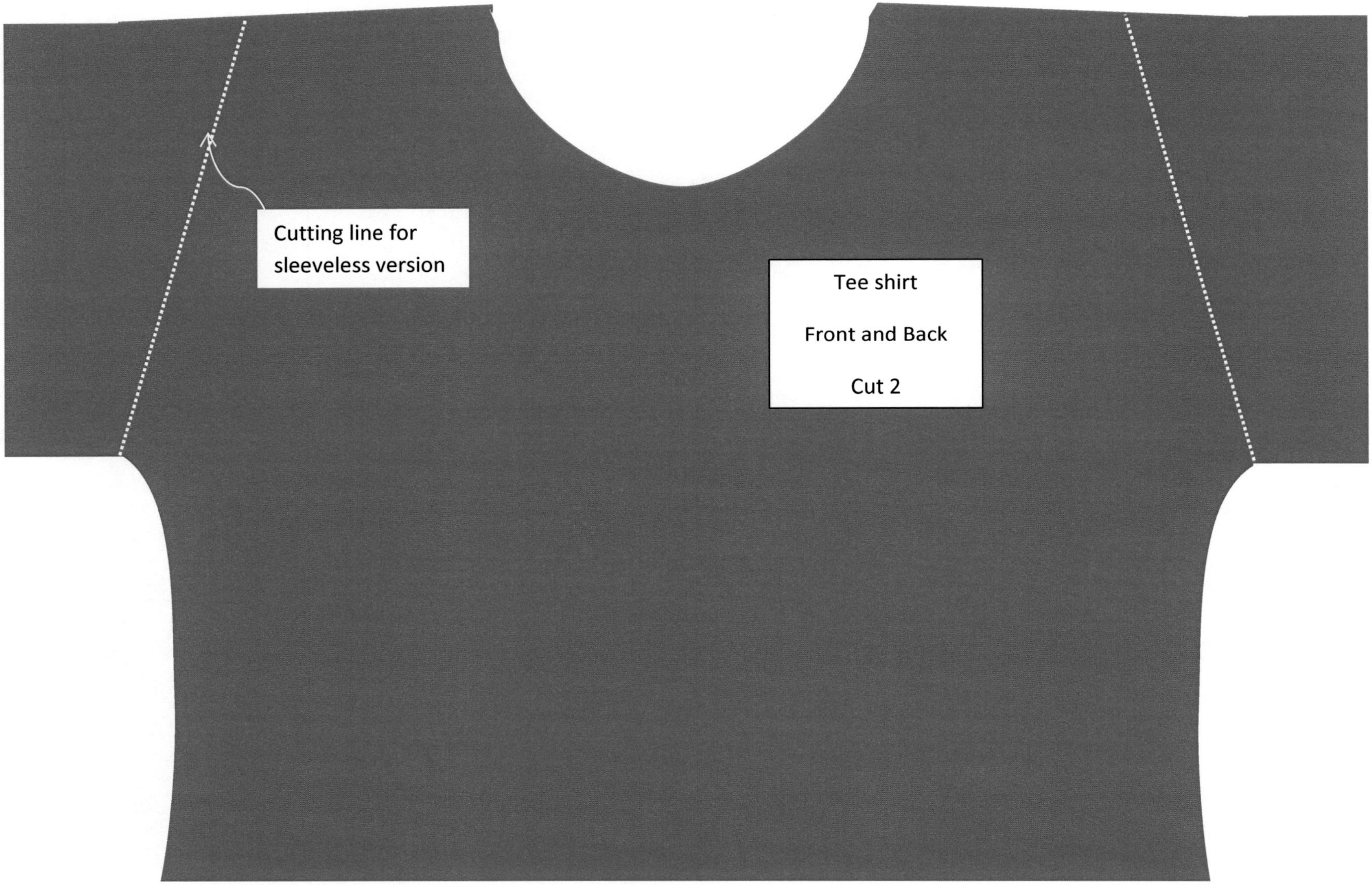

Tee shirt

Front and Back

Cut 2

Cutting line for sleeveless version

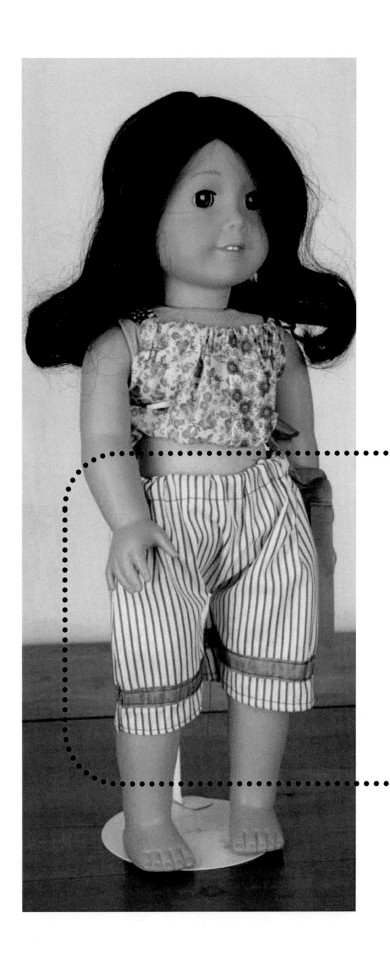

Surfer Shorts

You will need:
- ¼ yd (m) of fabric
- 1.5 yds (m) of ½-inch wide ribbon

Large safety pin

Skill Level

Surfer Shorts

Draw the shorts pattern piece on the RIGHT side of two pieces of fabric. Position the ribbon as shown on the fabric. Pin. Stitch in place.

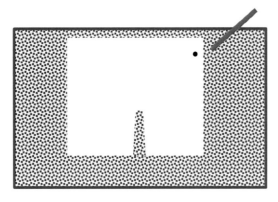 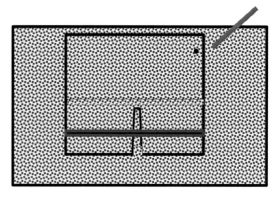

Cut out the shorts

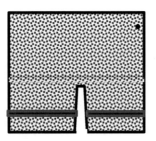

Hem the bottom edge of each leg. Fold a ¼-inch hem. Press. Fold a second ½-inch hem. Press. Pin. Stitch in place.

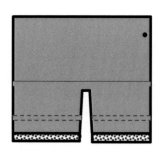

Put the right sides of the shorts together. Pin ONE side seam. Stitch in place.

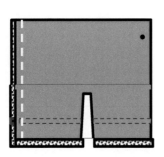

Clip each side seam at the dot. Sew down the top of each side seam as shown.

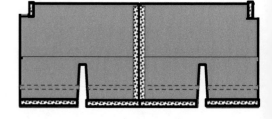

Make the casing. Fold a narrow ¼-inch hem across the waist of the shorts. Fold a second ¾-inch hem. Press. Stich in place.

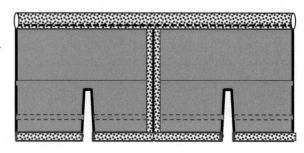

Sew the remaining side seam to just below the casing.

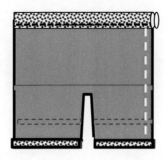

Sew the in-seam. Match the center of the shorts and the bottom of the legs. Pin. Stitch in place making a large, square U as shown. Clip carefully into the corners. Turn right side out. Press.

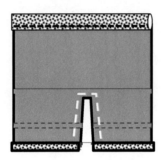

Grab your ribbon. Attach the ribbon to a large safety pin. Insert the ribbon into the casing.

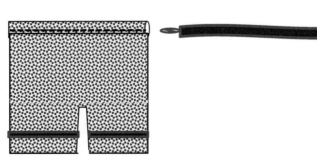

Try the shorts on your doll. Tie the ribbon into a bow and cut away the excess. That's it!

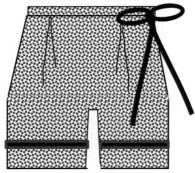

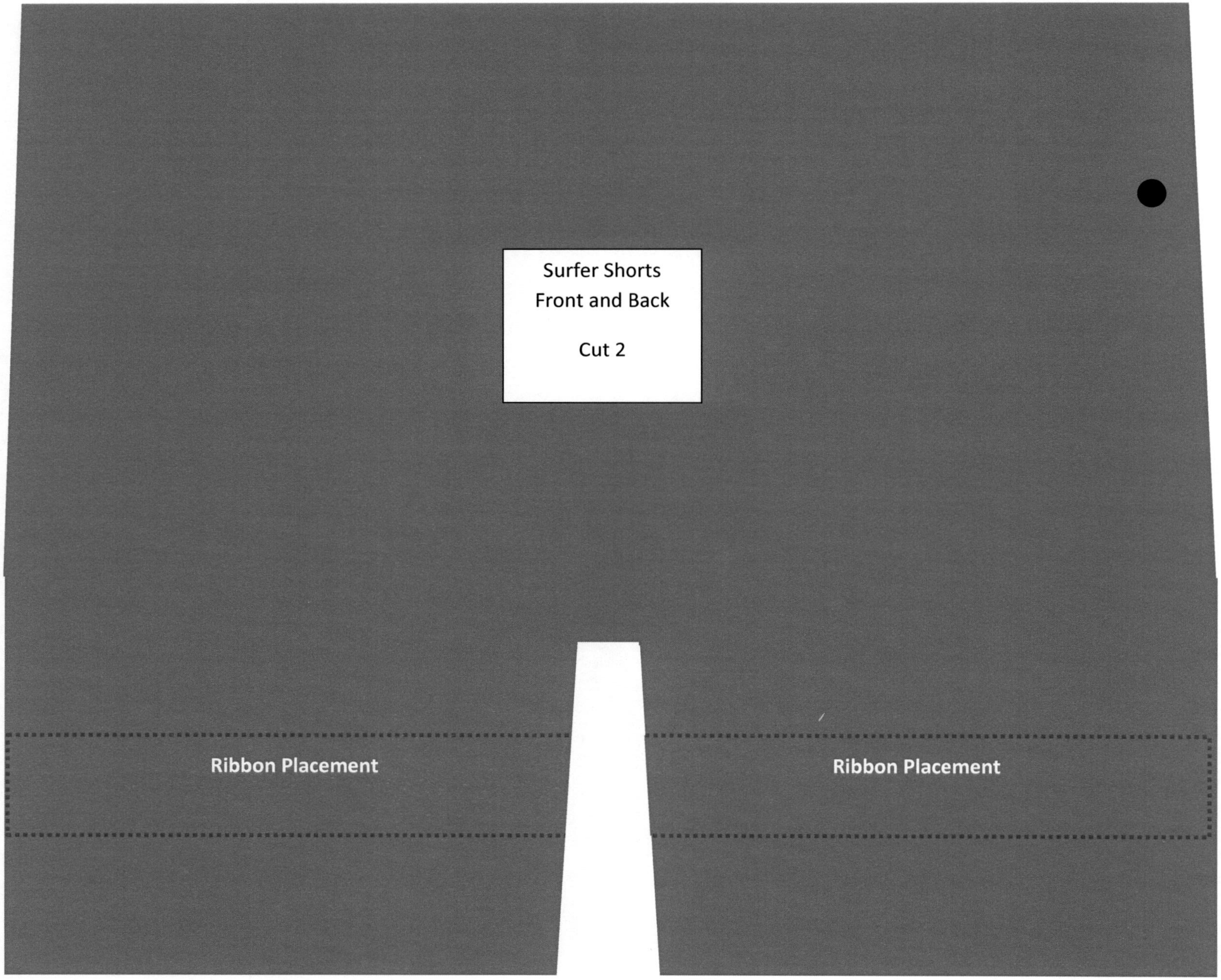

Surfer Shorts
Front and Back

Cut 2

Ribbon Placement

Ribbon Placement

Bow Tie Pencil Skirt

You will need:
- One ¼ yd (m) of fabric
- One large safety pin

Skill Level

Bow Tie Drawstring Skirt

Stack your fabric with the right sides together. Cut the skirt front and back 7" x 6.5" and tie 20"x 2".

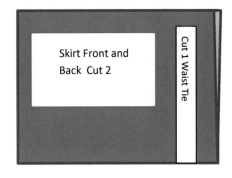

Sew the side seam.

Put the right sides of the skirt together. Pin ONE side seam. Stitch in place.

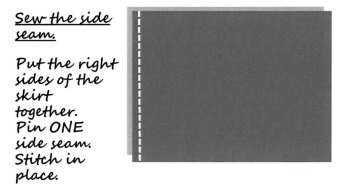

Make the casing. Fold a narrow ¼-inch hem at the top 2 inches of the remaining side seam as shown.

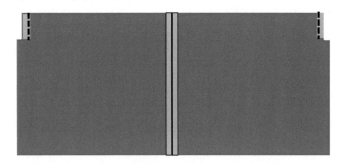

Fold a narrow ¼-inch hem across the waist. Fold a second ¾-inch hem. Press. Stich in place.

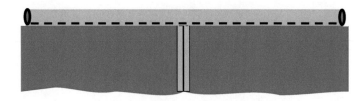

Finish the remaining side seam. Sew the remaining side seam to just below the casing.

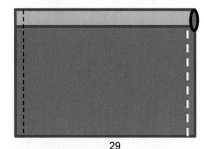

<u>Make the hem.</u> Turn a double ½-inch hem. Press. Stitch in place.

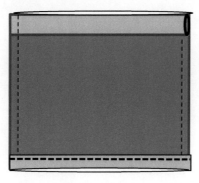

Retrieve the tie. Fold in one of the short edges of the tie as shown. Press. Fold the tie in half lengthwise. Stitch along the remaining short edge and then along the long edges with a 1/4-inch seam. Use a chopstick to turn the tie right side out. Stitch the open edge closed.

Attach the tie to a large safety pin. Insert the tie into the casing. Tie in a bow. If the tie is very long, you can cut off the excess and tie a knot at each end of the tie.

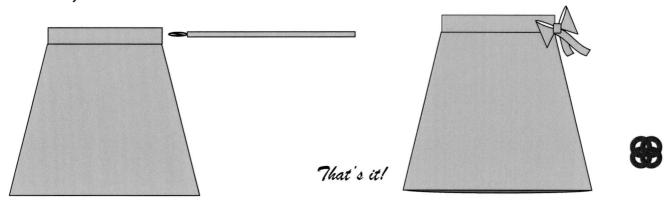

That's it!

Add a raw edge pocket and decorative stitching at the hem if you'd like!

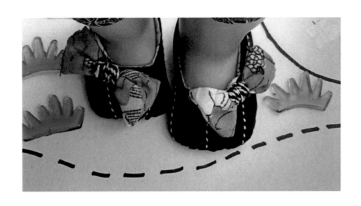

City Flats

You will need:

- One 7"x7" square of outside fabric
- One 7" x 7" fabric of lining fabric
- One small piece of interfacing for the sole

Skill Level

Layout: Cut out the Shoe Upper pattern piece (p.45). Stack your fabric with the right sides together. Trace the shoe upper on the fabric.

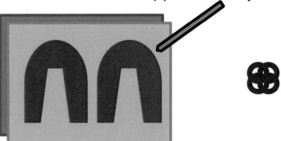

Stitch around the upper leaving one end open as shown.

Cut out the uppers leaving a small, 1/8-inch seam allowance. Snip the inside corners. Turn the uppers right side out with a chopstick. Smooth the curved front.

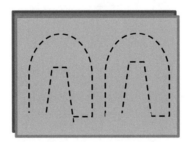

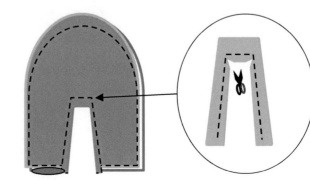

Turn the edges of the opening inward and stitch closed.

Set your machine to the widest zigzag stitch and a stitch length of about 20 stitches per inch. Bring the two back edges together and stitch in place. The stitch should be on both edges to connect the back of the shoe. Or, sew the back together by hand with the ladder stitch.

Make the sole of the shoe – follow the instructions for the City Sandal on page 10. Do not make the ribbon loop, just stitch the back opening on the sole of the shoe closed.

Position the upper so that the back of the upper is centered at the midpoint of the back edge of the sole and the center front of the upper is over the midpoint of the front of the sole. Pin. Attach the upper shoe to the sole using the ladder stitch. Begin at the center back. At the front of the shoe you will need to ease the upper to fit the sole. This is simple to do because the ladder stitch can do the easing for you! Make the stitch on the upper a little bit longr than the stitch on the sole. When you pull the thread, you will find that the upper fits neatly onto the sole!

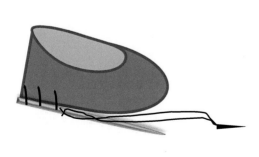 

That's it! You have created a fully reversible City Flat. Add a cute bow if you'd like.

Drawstring Croppie Top

You will need:

- Two 5" x 4" pieces of contrasting fabric
- One 15 inch piece of 1/2 –inch ribbon

One Large Safety Pin

Skill Level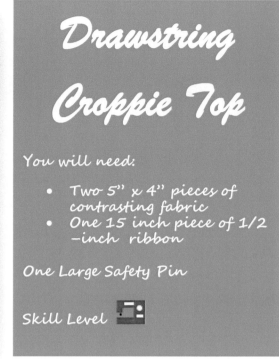

Drawstring Crop Top

Cut 4 rectangles of fabric. The fabric can be the same or contrasting.

Finish all 4 sides of each piece by stitching a narrow ¼-inch hem.

 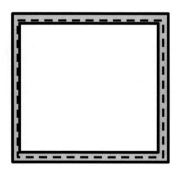

Sew the two contrasting pieces together.

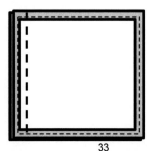

Drawstring Casing:

Fold a ½-inch hem to make the casing along the edge of the top. Stitch in place. Repeat for the back.

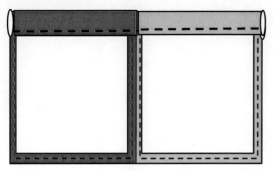

Completing the top.

Pin the side seams with the right sides together. Stitch 1.5 inches below the casing to the bottom of the tank

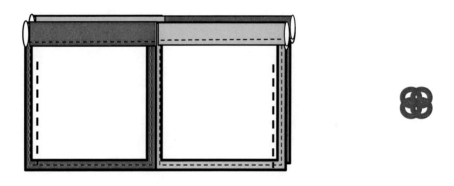

.

Cut a 12-inch length of 3/8- inch wide ribbon. Or make your own strap.

To make a strap, cut a 13-inch x 1.5 inch piece of fabric. Fold and sew along the raw edge. Turn right sides out with a safety pin or other turning tool. Tuck in the raw edges and stich in place.

Insert the strap through the back casing and into the front casing. Try on your doll. Sew the ends of the strap together or tie the strap on one shoulder.

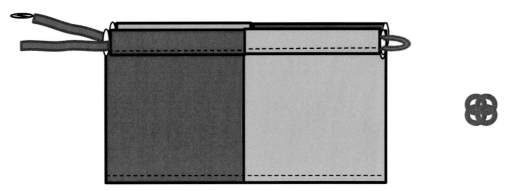

That's it!

*** This can be made as a croppie tank, a waist (cut fabric to 5"x5") or hip length tank (5"x6"), a thigh-length tunic (5"x7") or an above the knee dress (5"x8"). ***

Raw-Edge Applique Jumper

You will need:

- 3/8 yd (m) of fabric. Choose a fabric that ravels to make a cute raw edge finish.
- One 6"x6" square of muslin for the applique
- Hook and Loop tape or Velcro

Black and Pink Fabric Pens or Crayons

Skill Level

Applique Jumper with Raw Edge Neckline

Cut out the Jumper front and Back.

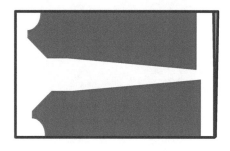

fold

Applique

Make the applique by tracing the image on lightweight muslin. If you are not able to see through the muslin, try copying and taping the image to a bright window and then putting the muslin on top. Color the image with a black fabric pin or crayon. Color the ears and cheeks with a pink fabric pen, water color pencil or crayon. If you think you will wash the jumper, set the color by pressing it with a warm iron.

Cut out the applique.

Stitch the applique onto the front of the jumper with a zigzag or straight stitch.

Finish the back edges. Turn under a narrow ¼-inch hem on each back edge of the jumper. Stitch in place

Finish the armholes. Fold a narrow ¼-inch hem along each armhole. Stitch in place

Make the shoulder seams. Match the front and backs of the jumper at the shoulder. Pin and stitch in place.

Finish the neckline. Staystitch around the neckline sewing about ¼ inch away from the edge. Cut the raw edge to 1/8

Sew one side seam.

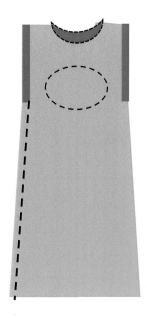

Make the Hem. Fold a ½-inch hem. Fold a second ½-inch hem. Stitch in place. OR staystitch ½ inch from the bottom edge of the jumper and pull out some of the crosswise threads to make the fringed edge.

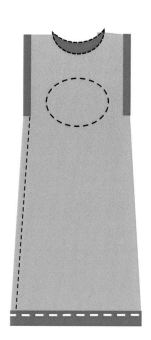

Sew the remaining side seam.

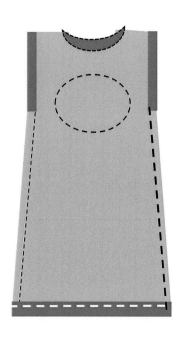

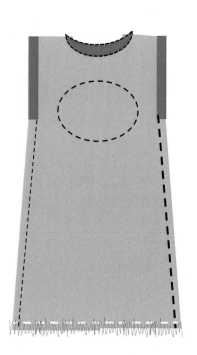

Try the jumper on your doll. Adjust the placement of the hook and loop tape. Stitch in place. That's it!

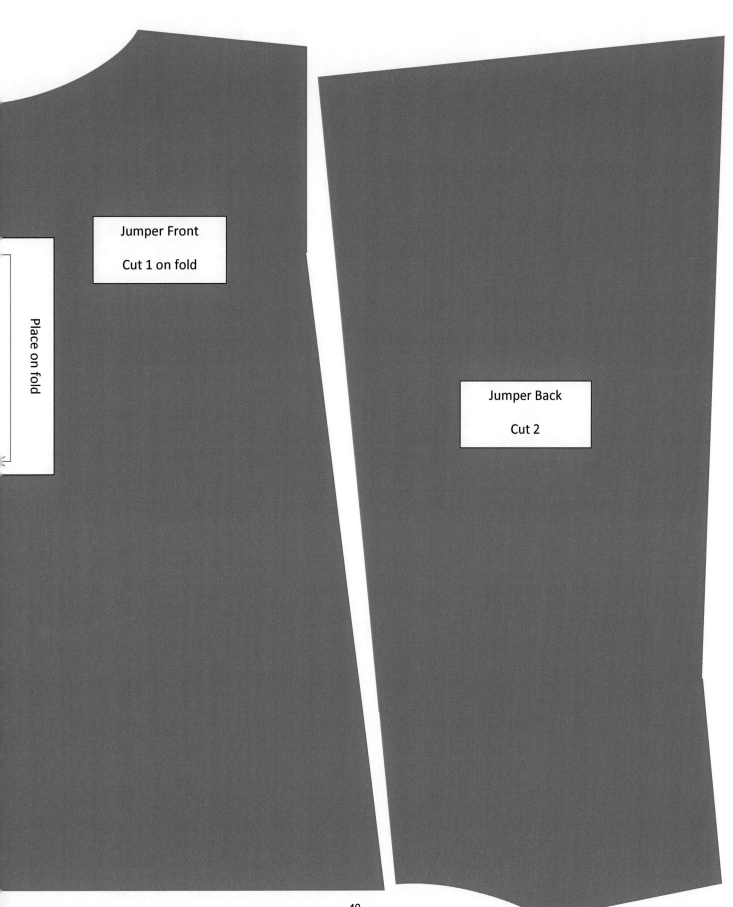

Applique Jumper Pattern Pieces
lengthen or shorten at lower edge

Jumper Front

Cut 1 on fold

Place on fold

Jumper Back

Cut 2

Hand Sew

Square Tee

and Skirt

You will need:

For the top
- One piece of fabric 7"x14"
- 3 snaps

For the skirt
- 2 pieces of fabric 10"x 7.5"
- One 11" piece of ½-inch wide elastic

Skill level: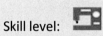

Hand Sew Square Tee and Skirt

These are so easy. With just a couple of pieces of fabric and a needle and thread, you can make a stylish doll shirt and skirt.

To make the shirt, cut two pieces of fabric 7-inches square.

Fold a narrow ¼-inch hem on all sides. Stitch the hems in place.

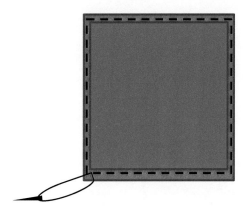 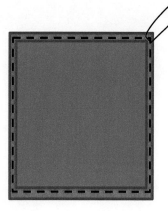

Make the shoulder seams by stitching a 1.5-inch long seam from each outer edge as shown.

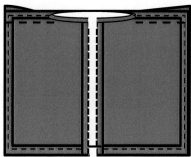

Make the side seams by stitching a 3.5-inch long seam from each bottom side edge as shown.

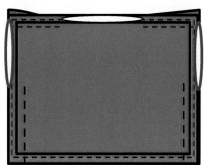

Turn the shirt right-sides out. Try the shirt on your doll. Position snaps. Sew the snaps on. That's it!

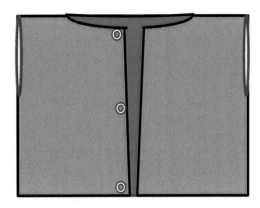

It's reversible! Wear as a shirt or a t-top.

Skirt

To make the skirt, cut two pieces of fabric 10 inches wide and 7.5 inches tall. This will be the front and back of the skirt.
Turn a narrow ¼-inch hem on one of the long edges of the skirt front and back.

Make the elastic casing. Turn a second 1-inch hem. Press. Thread a needle with a double strand of thread knotted at the end. Sew the casing in place. Repeat for the skirt back.

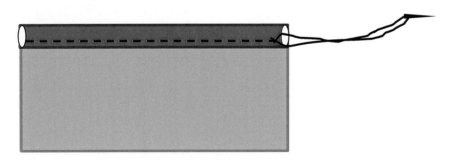

Grab your elastic. Cut the elastic into two 5½ inch pieces. Attach the elastic to a large safety pin and insert the elastic into the casing.

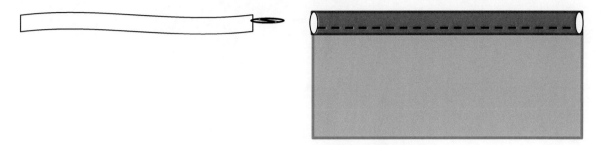

Sew the elastic securely at each end of the casing.

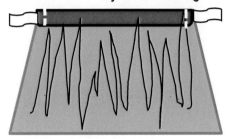

Put the skirt front and back with the right sides together. Stitch the side seams. Sew through all layers of the elastic. Knot off. Cut away the excess elastic.

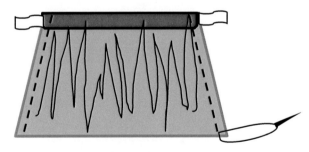

Fold a 1/4-inch hem at the bottom of the skirt. Fold a second 1/4-inch hem. Sew in place.
That's it!

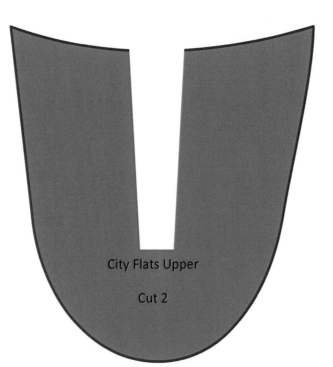

City Flats Upper

Cut 2

Sandal and Flats
Sole

Cut 4

69117233R00027

Made in the USA
San Bernardino, CA
11 February 2018